# The 4 Ingredient Kid Friendly Cookbook

### Over 50 Easy to Prepare Recipes That Kids Will Love!

by

Sherry Day

Copyright 2016
Sherry Day


ISBN-13: 978-1530345540
ISBN-10: 1530345545

# BREAKFAST

## RED, WHITE AND BLUE PARFAIT

This colorful breakfast provides a healthy start to a busy day!

- ✓ 1 cup plain Greek yogurt
- ✓ 1 cup granola
- ✓ 1 cup strawberries, chopped
- ✓ 1 cup blueberries

Divide the strawberries into four servings and place half of each serving on the bottom of 4 parfait cups. Spoon some yogurt over the strawberries. Divide the blueberries into four servings and place half of each serving over the yogurt mixture. Continue layering until all of the ingredients are used.

**VARIATION:** Combine 1 cup of vanilla yogurt with 1 cup of chopped pineapple, 1 cup of chopped peaches and 1 cup of granola. Follow the directions stated above.

Also try combining 1 cup of peach yogurt with 1 cup of chopped peaches, 1 cup of chopped pears and 1 cup of granola. Follow the directions stated above.

Serves 4

## FRUITY GRANOLA

Granola provides more fiber than most cereals, and requires no additional sweeteners.

- ✓ 2 cups old fashioned rolled oats
- ✓ 1 cup raisins
- ✓ 1/3 cup honey
- ✓ ½ cup raw sunflower seeds

Pre Heat oven to 300 degrees F.

Combine the rolled oats, sunflower seeds and honey in a large bowl, mixing well. Add a teaspoon of water of needed.

Bake for 10-12 minutes or until a light golden color. Turn at least once through the baking process. Remove from the oven, flip with a spatula and allow granola to cool for a couple minutes. Add the raisins, mixing well, and store cooled granola in a clean, airtight container.

Use within two weeks.

**VARIATION:** Combine 1/3 cup of maple syrup with ½ cup of unsweetened shredded coconut, 1 cup chopped, dried cranberries and 2 cups old fashioned rolled oats. Follow the directions as stated above, being sure to add the cranberries and coconut after the granola is cooked.

Serves 8-10

## CREAMY STRAWBERRY BREAKFAST TREATS

Quick and easy, and oh so delicious! Your kids will think it's a special morning when you prepare these sweet and delicious breakfast treats. I like to serve these delicious morning treats with the crock pot oatmeal.

- ✓ 8 oz pkg. crescent rolls
- ✓ 1-2 Tbs. milk
- ✓ 4 Tbs. strawberry jam
- ✓ 4 oz. cream cheese (softened)

Pre-heat oven to 375 degrees F.

Unroll the dough and press triangles together to form two rectangles. Combine the cream cheese and milk together until well blended. Spread mixture evenly onto each rectangle, leaving an inch border on all sides. Spread the jam evenly over cream cheese mixture and roll each rectangle into a log. Cut each log into one-inch slices. Place two inches apart from each other on a baking sheet, and bake for 12-15 minutes. Remove from oven and allow to stand for a couple minutes before serving.

**VARIATION:** Replace the strawberry jam with ¼ cup of cooked, crumbled sausage, and the cream cheese with ½ cup of shredded Monterey Jack cheese.

Serves 4-6

## CINNAMON SAUSAGE ROLLS

This delicious breakfast has your mouth watering by the time it comes out of the oven. The kids will love the combination of cinnamon rolls, sausage and maple icing, and you will love the adoration you will receive every time you make this recipe!

- ✓ 1 container (17.5 oz.) cinnamon rolls
- ✓ 10 fully cooked pork sausage links
- ✓ 10 toothpicks
- ✓ 1/3 cup maple syrup

Pre-heat oven to 350 degrees F.

Spray a baking sheet with cooking spray. Separate the dough slices and cut each slice in half. Wrap one slice around one piece of sausage. Secure each roll with a toothpick. Place each roll onto a baking sheet 3 inches apart and bake for 12-15 minutes, or until each roll is a golden color. Remove from oven and allow to set for about 5 minutes.

Meanwhile, combine the syrup with the icing, mixing well. Serve with warm cinnamon sausage rolls.

**VARIATION:** Replace the pork sausage links with 10 fully cooked turkey sausage links.

Serves 4-6

## CROCK POT OATMEAL

There is nothing like waking up to the smells of a hot breakfast. This easy-to-prepare meal provides the fiber and nutrition that little ones need for a busy day.

- ✓ 1 ½ cups dried cranberries
- ✓ 1 cup steel cut oatmeal
- ✓ ½ cup of half and half
- ✓ 4 cups of water

Before bedtime, combine the cranberries with the oatmeal, half and half and water in a crock pot set on low. Cook the oatmeal for 6-8 hours.

In the morning, you will wake up to a delicious, hot breakfast!

**VARIATION:** Replace the dried cranberries with 1 ½ cups of raisins.

Serves 4

## BREAKFAST EGG FLORENTINE SANDWICH

This approach to preparing poached eggs is much easier than the way my mother used to do it. I am sure she would have loved this recipe!

- ✓ 6 eggs
- ✓ ½ cup fresh spinach
- ✓ ½ cup shredded cheddar cheese
- ✓ 6 whole wheat English muffins
- ✓ Water

Pre-heat oven to 350 degrees F.

Pour about ½ to 1 tablespoon of water into each muffin cup. Crack an egg and place each egg into the prepared muffin cup. Drop a small handful of spinach over each egg, pushing spinach down into the egg.

Bake for 8-10 minutes, or until eggs are cooked to desired consistency.

Meanwhile, toast the English muffins and layer cheddar cheese on the bottom of each English muffin. Remove the eggs with a slotted spoon and place an egg over the cheese on each English muffin.

**VARIATION:** Replace the spinach with ½ cup chopped tomato, the cheddar cheese with 6 slices of American cheese, and the whole wheat English muffin with white English muffins. Follow the directions stated above.

Serves 6

# SNACKS FROM THE OVEN

## CHEESE STICKS

No need to buy prepackaged cheese sticks when you can make your own at a fraction of the cost.

- ✓ 1 pkg. (12 sticks) of String Cheese
- ✓ ½ cup plus 2 Tbs. Italian Bread Crumbs
- ✓ 1 egg, beaten
- ✓ 2-3 Tbs. flour

Cut each stick of string cheese in half. Place cheese in the freezer on wax paper for a few minutes. Beat the egg and place it in one bowl, place the flour in a second bowl, and the bread crumbs in a third bowl. Remove a few cheese sticks from the freezer. Dip one stick in the flour, followed by the egg mixture, and finish by dipping into the breadcrumbs. Place cheese sticks on a baking sheet and continue the process until finished. Place the cheese sticks back into the freezer for a couple more minutes.

Pre-heat oven to 400 degrees F.

Bake cheese sticks for 8 to 10 minutes, or until a golden color.

**VARIATION:** Replace the Italian bread crumbs with ½ cup plus 2 Tablespoons of Panko bread crumbs, and the flour with 2-3 Tablespoons whole wheat flour. Follow the directions stated above.

Makes 24 cheese sticks.

## ZUCCHINI FRIES

This is a healthy substitution for regular French fries. These fries are best served with Ranch dressing.

- ✓ 2 medium zucchini, unpeeled
- ✓ 1/2 cup Italian Bread Crumbs
- ✓ ½ cup shredded Parmesan cheese
- ✓ 1 egg, beaten

Pre-heat oven to 425 degrees F. Spray a baking sheet with non-stick cooking spray.

Slice the zucchini in half and then into 3 inch strips. Combine the bread crumbs and Parmesan cheese in a medium bowl, and the beaten egg in a separate bowl. Dip the zucchini strips into the egg mixture, and then into the bread crumb mixture. Place the zucchini fries on the prepared baking sheet.

Bake for 25-30 minutes, or until fully cooked. Remove from the oven and allow to stand for a couple minutes before serving/

**VARIATION:** Replace the zucchini with 4-5 large carrots, the Italian bread crumbs with 1/2 cup of Panko bread crumbs, and the Parmesan cheese with ½ cup of grated Ramano cheese. Follow the directions stated above.

Serves 4-6

## PIGS IN A BLANKET

This is a perfect afternoon snack for the whole family, but you may want to double the batch!

- ✓ 8 oz. container of crescent rolls
- ✓ 24 mini hot dogs
- ✓ Mustard and ketchup for dipping

Pre-heat oven to 375 degrees F.

Cut each crescent roll into thirds. Place the hot dogs on the largest side of the crescent roll and roll up until the roll is wrapped around each hot dog. Place, seam side down, on an ungreased cookie sheet.

Bake for 12 to 15 minutes, or until a golden color.

Serve with Mustard and Ketchup for dipping.

**VARIATION:** Replace the mini hot dogs with 24 mini sausage links, and the mustard and ketchup with barbecue sauce. Follow the directions stated above.

For Tangy Pigs in a Blanket, spread a little Dijon mustard onto the crescent roll before wrapping around the hot do or sausage.

Serves 4-6

## SWEET POTATO FRIES

Sweet potatoes are a delicious source of a variety of vitamins including vitamin A, B6 and C. They are also a good source of fiber, niacin, potassium and manganese.

- ✓ 4 medium sweet potatoes, peeled
- ✓ 1/3 – 1/2 cup olive oil
- ✓ 1/3 cup sea salt
- ✓ Ketchup or Ranch dressing for dipping

Pre-heat oven to 425 degrees F.

Slice the sweet potatoes in half, into 4 inch long slices, and then into 1/2 inch wide slices. Toss the fries in the olive oil and season with salt. Place the fries in a single, even layer on a non-stick baking sheet. Bake for 15 minutes, flip all of the fries, and continue baking for another 15 minutes, or until fully cooked. Remove from the oven and serve immediately.

**VARIATION:** Replace the sweet potatoes with 4 white potatoes, add 1-2 teaspoons of cayenne pepper to the sea salt, and replace the ketchup with tartar sauce for dipping. Follow the directions stated above.

Serves 6

## TEXAS STYLE PIZZA

This is a change from regular pizza. The kids will want to help you make this because they can get creative and add additional toppings. Best if served with Marinara sauce or Ranch dressing for dipping.

- ✓ 6 pieces frozen Texas Toast
- ✓ 1 small can or jar of pizza sauce
- ✓ 2 cups shredded Mozzerella cheese
- ✓ 25-30 pepperoni pieces

Pre-heat oven to 425 degrees F.

Place the frozen Texas toast on an ungreased baking sheet.

Bake for about two minutes, flip, and bake for another 2 minutes. Remove from oven, top with the pizza sauce, cheese and pepperoni pieces.

Return to the oven and bake for and additional 3-5 minutes.

**VARIATION:** Replace the Mozzarella cheese with 2 cups of shredded Cheddar cheese, and the pepperoni pieces with ½ to ¾ cup of chopped ham. Follow the directions stated above.

Serves 4-6

## SPINACH AND CHEESE BITES

Moms and Dads everywhere enjoy a moment's satisfaction when they see their kids eating spinach and enjoying it. These delicious bites are loaded with vitamins and nutrients, and are a nice change from packaged snacks.

- ✓ 1 cup fresh spinach leaves
- ✓ 1 ½ cups seasoned breadcrumbs, divided
- ✓ 2 eggs, beaten
- ✓ ½ cup shredded cheddar cheese

Pre-heat oven to 350 degrees F. Coat a baking sheet with non-stick cooking spray.

Place the spinach in a food processor and pulse until finely chopped. If you do not have a food processor, hand chop the spinach.

Combine the eggs, chopped spinach, cheese and ½ cup of breadcrumbs, mixing well. Place the remaining breadcrumbs in a smaller bowl. Roll the spinach mixture into 2-inch balls. Roll each ball in the breadcrumbs and place onto the prepared baking sheet. Press down a little with the back of a large spoon onto each ball. Bake for 18-23 minutes, turning the balls once. Remove from the oven and allow to sit for a couple minutes before serving.

**VARIATION:** Replace the breadcrumbs with 1 ½ cups of Panko bread crumbs, and the shredded cheddar cheese with ½ cup of shredded Mozzarella cheese. Follow the directions stated above.

Serves 4-6

# SNACKS ON THE GO

### RANCH OYSTER CRACKERS

This timeless recipe is great for traveling or as a snack for large parties.

- ✓ 1 bag of oyster crackers (don't buy the cheap ones!)
- ✓ ¼ cup extra virgin olive oil
- ✓ 1 (1 oz.) envelope of ranch dressing mix
- ✓ 1 tsp. dried dill

Pre-heat oven to 250 degrees F.

Combine all of the ingredients in a large bowl, mixing well. Transfer to a large ungreased baking sheet.

Bake for 20 minutes, flipping crackers about 2 or 3 times during the baking process.

Allow to cool before storing in a clean, airtight container.

**VARIATION:** Replace the ranch dressing mix with a package of taco seasoning, and the dried dill with 1 teaspoon Italian seasoning. Follow the directions stated above.

## PUPPY CHOW

This is a recipe that never gets old. The kids will love this snack during long car rides or on long trips where yummy snacks are a must!.

- ✓ 9 cups crispy rice cereal squares
- ✓ 1 cup semi-sweet chocolate chips
- ✓ ½ cup creamy peanut butter
- ✓ 1 ½ to 2 cups confectioners sugar
- ✓ Large plastic bag

Melt the chocolate chips in a medium saucepan over low heat. Add the peanut butter and mix until well blended. When the peanut butter is melted, remove from heat, fold in the cereal and stir until all of the cereal is coated. Pour the confectioner's sugar in the large plastic bag, add the cereal and shake well, making sure that all of the cereal is evenly coated.

Pour the mix onto a large baking sheet in a single layer and allow to dry before storing in a clean, airtight container.

**VARIATION:** Replace the semi-sweet chocolate chips with 1 cup of dark chocolate chips and the peanut butter with 1/2 cup of hazelnut butter. Follow the directions stated above.

Serves 8-10

## PARMESAN PITA WEDGES

Healthy and delicious snack that kids love, these Parmesan Pita Wedges will win over the pickiest eater!

- ✓ 6-inch whole-wheat pita, split
- ✓ ¼ cup grated Parmesan cheese
- ✓ 1 Tbs. butter, melted
- ✓ ¼ tsp. dried oregano

Pre-heat oven to 375 degrees F.

Cut the pita bread into triangles.

Brush each triangle with the melted butter, sprinkle with the Parmesan cheese and top with the dried oregano.

Transfer to a baking sheet and bake for 4-5 minutes or until a golden color.

**VARIATION:** Replace with whole-wheat pita bread with white pita bread, the Parmesan cheese with ¼ cup of Asiago cheese, and the dried oregano with Italian seasoning. Follow the directions stated above.

Serves 6

# FAVORITE TRAIL MIX

Trail Mix is a favorite in my house because it's so easy to make and kids love it! Even better, they love to help make this easy and delicious snack.

- ✓ 1 cup roasted, salted, shelled peanuts
- ✓ 1 cup semi-sweet chocolate chips
- ✓ 1 cup roasted & salted shelled sunflower seeds
- ✓ 1 cup raisins

Combine all of the ingredients and store in a clean, airtight container.

**VARIATION:** Combine together 1 cup each of cashews, chopped dried pineapple, shredded coconut and banana chips. Follow the directions stated above.

For a Hawaiian mix, combine together 1 cup each of macadamia nuts, white chocolate chips, dried pineapple chunks, and unsweetened coconut. Follow the directions stated above.

Serves 4-6

## CHEDDAR CHEESE CRACKERS

Don't buy cheese crackers loaded with preservatives when you can make your own. The entire household will love these tasty little treats!

- ✓ 2 cups extra sharp cheddar cheese, grated
- ✓ 1/2 cup unsalted butter
- ✓ 1 1/2 cups unbleached flour
- ✓ 1/2 tsp. sea salt

Preheat oven to 350 degrees F.

Combine the flour and salt in a small bowl and set aside. Cream together the butter with the cheese. Add the flour to the cheese mixture and mix well. Roll the dough into 1-inch balls and place onto an ungreased cookie sheet. Flatten with the palm of your hand or the bottom of a glass and press a criss-cross pattern across the top of the cracker with a fork.

Bake for 12-15 minutes until golden. Allow to cool before transferring from the baking sheet. Store in a clean, air-tight container.

**VARIATION**: Replace the cheddar cheese with 2 cups of Parmesan cheese, and the sea salt with 1 tsp. of Italian seasoning. Follow the directions stated above.

Serves 4-6

## PEANUT BUTTER BANANA BARS

These peanut butter banana bars are not only delicious, but are a healthy alternative to cookies and other sweets.

- ✓ 4 medium bananas, mashed
- ✓ 2 cups old fashioned rolled oats
- ✓ ½ cup creamy peanut butter
- ✓ 1/2 cup chopped walnuts

Spray the bottom of a 9x13-inch glass baking pan with non-stick cooking spray.

Preheat the oven to 350 degrees F.

Mix together the bananas, oats, and peanut butter. Spread the dough evenly in the prepared baking pan. Sprinkle with the chopped walnuts.

Bake for 18-20 minutes. Allow to cool for a couple minutes before cutting into bars. Store in a clean, airtight container in the refrigerator.

**VARIATION:** Replace the peanut butter with ½ cup of cashew butter, and the chopped walnuts with ½ cup of chopped cashews. Follow the directions stated above.

Serves 6-8

# HARVEST FRUIT DISHES

## PEACH SALAD

Do you have fresh peaches and you're not sure what to do with them? Add three additional items and you have a healthy lunch or snack.

- ✓ 4 fresh peaches, peeled and cut in half
- ✓ 8 oz. cream cheese, softened
- ✓ 1 cup finely chopped walnuts
- ✓ Lettuce leaves

Place the lettuce leaves evenly on 8 plates. Combine the cream cheese with the walnuts, mixing well. Drop about a tablespoon of the cream cheese mixture into the center of each peach, spreading evenly. Place a peach on each lettuce leave.

**VARIATION:** Replace with fresh peaches with 4 fresh pears, the cream cheese with 1 cup of shredded cheddar cheese, and the walnuts with 1 cup of finely chopped pecans. Follow the directions stated above.

Serves 8

## STRAWBERRY DELIGHT

I take this dish to summer family picnics, and always come home with an empty bowl!

- ✓ 8 oz. Whipped Topping
- ✓ 2 cups fresh, chopped strawberries
- ✓ 1 cup finely chopped walnuts
- ✓ 1 angel food cake, broken or cut into one-inch pieces

Combine the whipped topping with the chopped strawberries, walnuts and angel food cake pieces. Mix until well combined.

Refrigerate for at least an hour before serving.

**VARIATION:** Replace the strawberries with 2 cups of raspberries and the walnuts with 1 cup of finely chopped pecans. Follow the directions stated above.

Serves 8-10

## PEAR SORBET

This is a good recipe to make when you have a bushel of fresh pears and aren't quite sure what to do with them!

- ✓ 5 pears, peeled and sliced
- ✓ ¾ cup apple juice
- ✓ 1/3 cup sugar
- ✓ 4 tsp. lemon juice

Combine all of the ingredients in a large saucepan over medium-high heat. When the mixture begins to boil, reduce the heat and simmer for about 10 minutes or until the pears are cooked through. Remove from heat and allow the mixture to cool for a couple of minutes.

Pour the mixture in a food processer or use a hand immersion blender and process for 2 minutes or until fully processed. Transfer to a 13 by 9-inch casserole dish and freeze for 4-5 hours, or until firm.

Before serving, process the mixture again, either in a food processer or using a hand immersion blender. Spoon into ice cream dishes and serve immediately.

**VARIATION:** Replace the pears with 5 peaches and the apple juice with ¾ cup of fresh orange juice. Follow the directions stated above.

Serves 4-6

# STRAWBERRY BANANA ICE CREAM

Your kids will love the combination of fresh fruit and cream. You may want to double the recipe, it disappears quickly!

- ✓ 4 medium bananas, cut into thirds
- ✓ 1 cup strawberries, hulled and halved
- ✓ 1 tsp. vanilla extract
- ✓ 4 Tbs. heavy cream

Combine the bananas with the strawberries, vanilla extract and cream in a food processor or blender, processing well.

Transfer the mixture to a 13 by 9-inch casserole dish and freeze for at least four hours or overnight.

**VARIATION:** Replace the bananas with 2 cups of raspberries and the strawberries with 1 cup of blueberries. Follow the directions stated above.

Serves 4

## FROZEN PEACH YOGURT

Not sure what to do with fresh peaches? This is the perfect recipe for fresh, summer peaches.

- ✓ 2 cups fresh peaches, chopped
- ✓ 1/2 cup plain Greek yogurt
- ✓ 2 Tbs. of honey
- ✓ 1/4 tsp. vanilla extract

Combine all of the ingredients in a food processor and blend until smooth and creamy.

Freeze for at least one hour before serving.

## VARIATIONS:

Combine 2 cups of fresh raspberries with ½ cup of vanilla yogurt, 2 Tbs. of maple syrup and ¼ tsp. of vanilla extract. Follow the directions stated above.

Combine 2 cups of chopped strawberries with ½ cup of strawberry yogurt, 2 Tbs. of maple syrup and ¼ tsp. of vanilla extract. Follow the directions stated above.

Serves 4

## FRUIT AND CHEESE KABOBS

What's not to love? Healthy, Delicious and Easy to Prepare sum up this creative snack.

- ✓ ½ cup blueberries
- ✓ 1 cup strawberries, halved
- ✓ 1 cup pineapple chunks
- ✓ 8 oz. cheddar cheese cut into one-inch cubes
- ✓ Wooden kabob skewers

Place the fruit and cheese on the wooden skewers and refrigerate until ready to serve.

You can get fancy with the cheese and slice it into shapes such as stars or hearts.

**VARIATION:** Place kiwi slices, cantaloupe chunks, seedless green grapes and Monterey Jack cheese cubes on the wooden skewers and place in the refrigerator until ready serve.

Serves 4-6

# KID-FRIENDLY SALADS

## SWEET CUCUMBER SALAD

I have never had a complaint with this cucumber salad, especially when you use garden fresh cucumbers!

- ✓ 2 cucumbers, peeled and thinly sliced
- ✓ ¼ cup sour cream
- ✓ 1 tsp. sugar
- ✓ 1 tsp. dried dill

Combine all of the ingredients in a medium bowl, mixing well.

Refrigerate for at least 30 minutes before serving.

**VARIATION:** Replace the sour cream with ¼ cup of plain Greek yogurt and the dried dill with 1 tsp. of fresh chives. Follow the directions stated above.

Serves 4

## MOM'S POTATO SALAD

This is our favorite potato salad, and is so easy to prepare. Be sure to double the recipe for large parties.

- ✓ 4 medium Russet potatoes; cooked, peeled and cubed
- ✓ 2 hard-boiled eggs, peeled and chopped
- ✓ 1/3 cup mayonnaise
- ✓ ¼ cup finely chopped green pepper

Combine all of the ingredients, mixing until well blended.

Refrigerate for at least an hour before serving. Stir well before serving, adding additional mayonnaise if needed.

**VARIATION:** Combine 5-6 small red-skin potatoes with ½ cup finely chopped radishes, ½ teaspoon dried dill and 1/3 cup of mayonnaise. Follow the directions stated above.

Serves 4-6

## PEANUT PEA SALAD

This is a great summer salad, and is delicious with burgers or sandwiches.

- ✓ 2 cups cooked peas
- ✓ 1 cup red Spanish peanuts
- ✓ ½ cup sour cream
- ✓ ½ cup mayonnaise

Combine the peas with the peanuts, sour cream and mayonnaise.

Refrigerate for at least 30 minutes before serving.

**VARIATION:** Combine 1 cup of chopped cashews with ½ cup of plain Greek yogurt, ½ cup of sour cream and 2 cups of small, raw broccoli pieces. Follow the directions stated above.

Serves 4-6

# SPAGHETTI SALAD

Delicious and easy, kids love eating spaghetti, whether it be hot or cold! Because there is no mayo in this salad, this is a good recipe to double up on and take to summer picnics.

- ✓ 1 pound spaghetti
- ✓ ¾ cup peeled and finely chopped carrots
- ✓ ¾ cup finely chopped tomato
- ✓ 1 bottle zesty Italian dressing

Cook the pasta according to package directions and drain.

Combine the cooked spaghetti with the carrots, tomato and Italian dressing, mixing well.

Refrigerate for at least an hour before serving. Mix well before serving.

**VARIATION:** Combine 1 pound of rotini pasta with ¾ cup of finely chopped green pepper, ¾ cup of finely chopped sweet red pepper and 1 bottle of Ranch dressing. Follow the directions stated above.

Serves 6

## BEAN SALAD

Everybody loves a good bean salad, especially one that is so quick and easy to prepare!

- ✓ 2 (15 oz.) cans tri-mixed beans, drained
- ✓ 1 cup cooked corn
- ✓ 3/4 cup chopped green pepper
- ✓ 1 bottle zesty Italian dressing

Combine the beans with the corn, green pepper and Italian dressing, mixing well.

Chill for at least one hour before serving.

**VARIATION:** Combine one can of black beans with one can of cannelli beans, ¾ cup chopped red onion, and 1 cup of sweet red pepper. Follow the directions stated above.

Serves 4-6

# TUNA PEA PASTA SALAD

This is still one of my favorite go-to salads. Make a double batch for summer picnics and be prepared for no left-overs!

- ✓ 12 oz. cooked macaroni pasta
- ✓ 2 cups cooked peas
- ✓ 5 oz. can chunk light tuna, drained
- ✓ ¾ cup mayonnaise

Cook the pasta according to package directions and drain.

Combine the cooked peas with the cooked pasta, tuna and mayonnaise, mixing well.

Chill for at least one hour before serving, being sure to stir well before serving. Add additional mayonnaise if needed.

**VARIATION:** Combine 12 oz. of cooked shell shaped pasta with a small, drained can of mushroom pieces, a can of drained, cooked chicken and ¾ cup of mayonnaise. Follow the directions stated above.

Serves 4-6

# FAVORITE PASTA

### TIMELESS FETTUCCINI

Everyone loves home-made fettuccini. Serve with a salad and rolls, and you have a delicious dinner!

- ✓ 1 pound fettuccine
- ✓ 1 cup cream
- ✓ ½ cup butter, softened
- ✓ ¾ cup Parmesan cheese, grated

Cook the pasta according to package directions and drain.

Combine the butter and cheese together in a medium saucepan over medium-high heat, stirring with a whisk. When the mixture begins to bubble, reduce the heat and simmer for a couple minutes, stirring with a whisk a couple of times.

Fold in the cooked noodles and mix until well blended. Serve immediately.

**VARIATION:** Replace the fettuccine with 1 pound of cooked spaghetti and the cream with 1 cup of Pecorino cheese. Follow the directions stated above.

Serves 4-6

# MAC AND CHEESE

This is a healthy alternative to box mixes and tastes just like Mom used to make!

- ✓ 2 cups elbow macaroni
- ✓ 2 cups milk
- ✓ 1 ½ cups shredded cheddar cheese
- ✓ 1 tsp. mustard powder

Combine the macaroni, milk and mustard powder in a medium saucepan over medium-high heat. When mixture begins to boil, reduce the heat and simmer for about 20 minutes, or until the macaroni is fully cooked. Be sure to stir often during the cooking process.

Remove from heat, add the cheddar cheese and mix until well blended.

**VARIATION:** Replace half of the shredded cheddar cheese with Parmesan cheese.

Serves 4-6

## CHEESY SPAGHETTI

Kids will love this quick and easy cheesy pasta dish.

- ✓ 1 pound spaghetti
- ✓ 1 cup Parmesan cheese, grated
- ✓ ¾ cup Ramano cheese, grated
- ✓ 2 Tbs. milk

Cook the pasta according to package directions and drain.

Combine the cheeses with the milk over medium-low heat, stirring well. Cook until the cheese is melted. Fold in the cooked pasta and stir until heated through. Remove from heat and serve immediately.

**VARIATIONS:** Replace the Ramano and Parmesan cheese with 2 cups of shredded cheddar cheese. Follow the directions stated above.

Serves 4-6

## BAKED SPAGHETTI

This is a hearty meal that the entire family with enjoy!

- ✓ 1 pound spaghetti
- ✓ 1 (25 oz) jar pasta sauce
- ✓ 1 ½ cups mozzarella cheese, grated
- ✓ 1 small can mushroom pieces, drained

Pre-heat oven to 325 degrees F.

Spray a 1.5 quart casserole dish with non-stick cooking spray.

Cook the pasta according to package directions and drain.

Combine the cooked spaghetti with the pasta sauce and mushroom pieces, mixing well. Transfer to the prepared casserole dish and top with cheese.

Bake for 20-30 minutes, or until cheese is melted.

**VARIATION:** Combine 1 pound of cooked and drained Angel Hair Pasta, 2 cups cooked, crumbled Italian sausage and 1 (25 oz.) jar of pasta sauce. Top with a combination of ¾ cup of Mozzarella and Parmesan cheese, following the directions stated above.

Serves 4-6

## CREAMY CHICKEN PASTA

This is a warm pasta salad that is perfect for a healthy lunch or light dinner. The best thing about this delicious dish is that it only takes a couple minutes to prepare!

- ✓ 4 cups cooked Rotelli pasta
- ✓ 2 cups cooked chicken, cut into bite-size pieces
- ✓ 1 ½ cups of cooked peas
- ✓ 1 (25 oz.) jar Alfredo sauce

Cook the pasta according to package directions and drain.

Combine the cooked pasta with the chicken and peas in a medium saucepan over medium-low heat. Stir in the and Alfredo sauce and stir until well blended.

Serve immediately.

**VARIATIONS:** Combine 4 cups of cooked and drained bow tie pasta with 2 cups of cooked and crumbled Italian sausage, 1 (25 oz.) jar of Marinara Sauce and a small can of drained mushroom pieces. Follow the directions stated above.

Serves 4-6

# FAVORITE TUNA CASSEROLE

This is a timeless recipe that never grows old. It's also an easy dish to freeze for a quick and easy meal.

- ✓ 12 oz. cooked butter noodles
- ✓ 2 cups frozen peas
- ✓ 5 oz. can chunk light tuna, drained
- ✓ 1 can cream of mushroom soup plus one can of water

Pre-heat oven to 350 degrees F. Spray a 9 by 9-inch baking dish with non-stick cooking spray.

Cook the pasta according to package directions and drain.

Combine the peas, tuna, soup and water; place in the prepared baking dish.

Bake for 30 minutes, remove from the oven and serve immediately.

**VARIATION:** Combine 12 oz. of cooked and drained shell shaped pasta, 2 cups of chopped and cooked ham (or canned ham), cheddar cheese soup with water and the frozen peas together, preparing as stated above.

Serves 4

# ONE DISH MEALS

## TATER TOT CASSEROLE

This is a fun casserole to make. It's so easy, the kids will want to help!

- ✓ 1 can cheddar cheese soup
- ✓ 1 can milk
- ✓ 1 cup sour cream
- ✓ 1 package of tater tots

Pre-heat oven to 350 degrees F. Spray a 13 by 9-inch baking dish with non-stick cooking spray.

Combine all of the ingredients in a large bowl and transfer to the prepared baking dish.

Bake for 1 hour or until fully cooked.

**VARIATION**: Combine a can of cream of mushroom soup with 1 can of milk, 1 cup of sour cream, a small can of drained mushrooms, and the package of tater tots. Follow the directions stated above.

Serves 4-6

# BAKED TORTILLINI

This is a delicious and filling dinner. A perfect meal for a cold winter's night!

- ✓ 1 lb. bulk pork sausage, cooked, drained & crumbled
- ✓ 2 (9 oz.) bags frozen cheese tortellini
- ✓ 1 jar (25 oz.) pasta sauce
- ✓ 2 cups Mozzarella cheese, shredded

Pre-heat oven to 350 degrees F. Spray a 13 by 9-inch casserole dish with non-stick cooking spray.

Cook the tortellini according to package directions and drain.

Combine the cooked sausage with the pasta sauce and tortellini. Place the mixture in the prepared casserole dish. Top evenly with the cheese.

Bake for 25 to 30 minutes, or until the cheese is melted.

**VARIATION:** Combine 1 lb. of cooked and crumbled turkey with 2 (9 oz.) bags of cheese ravioli, 1 jar (25 oz.) of marinara sauce, and 2 cups of a combination of grated Parmesan and Ramano cheese. Follow the directions stated above.

Serves 4-6

## AWARD WINNING GOULASH

I won a recipe contest for this recipe years ago. It's a dish that my mother used to make a lot, and is so easy to prepare and versatile.

- ✓ 1 pound elbow macaroni
- ✓ 1 pound cooked and crumbled ground beef, drained
- ✓ 1 (25 oz.) jar pasta sauce
- ✓ 2 cups shredded cheddar cheese, divided

Pre-heat oven to 350 degrees F. Coat a 9 by 9-inch baking dish with non-stick cooking spray.

Cook the pasta according to package directions and drain.

Combine the cooked macaroni, cooked beef, pasta sauce and half of the cheese, mixing well. Transfer to the prepared baking dish and top with remaining cheese.

Bake for 15-20 minutes, or until thoroughly cooked.

**VARIATION:** Combine 1 pound of cooked and drained rigatoni pasta with 1 pound of cooked and crumbled ground turkey, 1 (25 oz.) jar of marinara sauce, and 2 cups shredded or cubed American cheese. Follow the directions stated above.

Serves 4-6

## BAKED CHICKEN PENNE

This is a delicious way to use up leftover chicken. The kids will eat it up!

- ✓ 2 cups cooked chicken, chopped
- ✓ 1 (25 oz.) jar pasta sauce
- ✓ 1 lb. Penne pasta
- ✓ 1 ½ cups Mozzarella cheese, grated

Pre-heat oven to 350 degrees F. Coat a 9 by 9-inch baking dish with non-stick cooking spray.

Cook the pasta according to package directions and drain.

Combine the cooked chicken with the pasta sauce, cooked pasta and 1 cup of cheese. Place in the prepared baking dish and sprinkle with remaining cheese.

Bake for 15-20 minutes or until cooked through.

**VARIATION:** Combine 2 cups of cooked chopped shrimp with 1 (25 oz.) jar of Alfredo sauce, 1 pound of cooked Fettuccini, and 1 cup of Mozzarella cheese. Follow the directions stated above.

Serves 4-6

## COTTAGE PIE

Healthy and delicious! This recipe incorporates meat, potatoes and vegetables into one well-rounded meal!

- ✓ 1 pound ground beef, cooked, drained and crumbled
- ✓ 3 cups prepared mashed potatoes
- ✓ 2 cups cooked peas
- ✓ ½ cup beef broth

Pre-heat oven to 350 degrees F. Coat a 9 by 9-inch baking dish with non-stick cooking spray.

Combine the cooked beef with the peas and beef broth, mixing until well combined. Transfer to the prepared baking dish and top evenly with mashed potatoes.

Bake for 20-25 minutes.

**VARIATION:** Combine 1 pound of cooked ground turkey or chopped turkey with 2 cups of a combination of peas and carrots and ½ cup of chicken broth together, mixing until well combined. Transfer to the prepared baking dish and top evenly with 3 cups mashed sweet potatoes. Follow the directions stated above.

Serves 4-6

# BAKED CHILI CHEESE DOGS

This is a delicious alternative to plain hot dogs.

- ✓ 2 (15 oz.) cans chili with beans
- ✓ 1 pkg. all beef hot dog
- ✓ 10 flour tortillas
- ✓ 2 cups shredded cheddar cheese

Pre-heat oven to 425 degrees F. Spray a 13 by 9-inch baking dish with non-stick cooking spray.

Pour one can of the chili on the bottom of the prepared baking dish. Roll a tortilla around each hot dog and place, seam side down, into the baking dish. Top the hot dogs with the other can of chili. Lastly, sprinkle the cheddar cheese evenly over the chili.

Bake for 30 minutes, remove from the oven and serve immediately.

**VARIATION:** Replace the beef hot dogs with 1 pkg. of turkey dogs and the shredded cheddar cheese with 2 cups of Monterey jack cheese. Follow the directions stated above.

Serves 6-8

# JUST FOR KIDS

### PIZZA CALZONES

There will be no complaints after you serve these cheese filled calzones!

- ✓ 1 (8 oz.) pkg. crescent rolls
- ✓ 1 cup pizza sauce, divided
- ✓ 4 cheese sticks, cut in half, lengthwise
- ✓ 3.5 oz. pkg. sliced pepperonis

Pre-heat oven to 350 degrees F.

Unroll the crescent triangles. Place a tablespoon of pizza sauce, a half stick of cheese and about 4-6 slices of pepperoni on each triangle. Carefully roll up each triangle, starting with the wide part of the roll. Place each roll seam-side down on a large baking sheet.

Bake for 10 to 14 minutes or until a golden color. Remove from the oven and serve with extra pizza sauce.

**VARIATION:** Replace the pizza sauce with spaghetti sauce and the sliced pepperonis with 1 cup of chopped cooked ham. Follow the directions stated above.

Serves 6-8

## HOT DOG MASH

I made this recipe when I was a teenager and the whole family loved it!

- ✓ 6 all beef hot dogs
- ✓ 1 – 1 ½ cup of prepared mashed potatoes
- ✓ 3 Tbs. sour cream
- ✓ 1 cup shredded cheddar cheese

Pre-heat oven to 325 degrees F.

Boil the hot dogs according to package directions. Combine the mashed potatoes with the sour cream, mixing well. Slice each hot dog down the middle about half-way through the hot dog. Spoon a generous portion of mashed potatoes evenly down the middle of each dog. Sprinkle the cheese over the mashed potatoes. Place the stuffed hot dogs in a shallow baking sheet.

Bake for 10-12 minutes or until heated through and the cheese is melted.

**VARIATION:** Replace the hot dogs with 6 cooked polish sausage, the mashed potatoes with 1 to 1 ½ cups of sauerkraut, and the cheddar cheese with 1 cup of shredded Swiss cheese. Follow the directions stated above. Place a dollop of Thousand Island dressing on each polish sausage before serving.

Serves 4-6

## BEAN AND WEINER BAKE

This is a hearty meal, perfect for autumn or winter.

- ✓ 16 oz. can pork and beans
- ✓ 1 pkg all beef hot dogs
- ✓ 7.5 oz. pkg. prepared refrigerated biscuits
- ✓ 1 cup shredded cheddar cheese

Pre-heat oven to 400 degrees F.

Cut the hot dogs into one-inch pieces. Place in boiling water and cook according to package directions. Remove from heat and drain.

Combine the hot dogs and pork and beans and transfer to a 8-inch baking dish. Arrange the biscuits over the bean mixture and sprinkle with the cheese.

Bake for 10-15 minutes, or until the biscuits are golden and baked through.

**VARIATION:** Replace the hot dogs with 3 cups of cooked and chopped pork, use 1 cup of shredded grated Monterey jack cheese instead of the cheddar, and follow the directions stated above.

Serves 4-6

## CORN DOG MUFFINS

The kids will love these fun-filled corn muffins!

- ✓ 2 (8.5 oz.) pkg. of corn muffin mix
- ✓ 1 pkg. of all beef hot dogs
- ✓ 2/3 cup of milk
- ✓ 2 eggs

Pre-heat oven to 400 degrees F.

Spray muffin tins with non-stick cooking spray.

Cut each hot dog into one-inch pieces

Combine the corn muffin mixes with the milk and eggs, mixing until well blended. Fill each muffin tin 2/3 full with the corn muffin mix. Place a hot dog piece in the center of each tin.

Bake for 15 minutes, or until fully cooked.

Remove from the oven and allow to stand for a couple minutes before serving.

**VARIATION:** Replace the hot dogs with mini sausage links. Follow the directions stated above.

Serves 4-6

## MINI PIZZAS

Kids love helping in the kitchen and this is the perfect recipe for little hands!

- ✓ 1 can (16.3 oz) prepared refrigerated biscuits
- ✓ 1 cup pizza sauce
- ✓ 8 oz. shredded mozzarella cheese
- ✓ 3.5 oz. sliced pepperoni

Pre-heat oven to 375 degrees F.

Coat a cookie sheet with non-stick cooking spray.

Unroll the biscuits and place on the prepared cookie sheet. Top each biscuit with 1-2 tablespoons of pizza sauce and cheese, and a few slices of pepperoni.

Bake for 12-15 minutes. Remove from the oven and serve immediately.

**VARIATION:** Replace the pizza sauce with 1 cup of spaghetti sauce, the mozzarella cheese with 1 cup of Monterey Jack cheese, and the peperoni with 1 cup chopped cooked ham or crumbled sausage. Follow the directions stated above.

Serves 4-6

## CHICKEN ENCHILADA BAKE

Not sure what to make for dinner? This is a quick and easy meal, and is sure to be a hit with the kids.

- ✓ 2 cups chopped, cooked chicken
- ✓ 1 (14 oz.) jar enchilada sauce
- ✓ 6 (6-inch) flour tortillas
- ✓ 2 cups shredded Monterey Jack cheese

Pre-heat oven to 375 degrees F. Coat a 9 by 9-inch baking dish with non-stick cooking spray.

In the prepared baking dish, layer one half of the enchilada sauce, 3 tortillas, 1 cup of chicken, 1 cup of cheese, and repeat layers.

Bake for 20 to 25 minutes. Remove from oven and serve immediately.

**VARIATION:** Replace the cooked chicken with 2 cups of cooked ham, and the Monterey Jack cheese with 2 cups of shredded sharp cheddar cheese. Follow the directions stated above.

Serves 4-6

# COOKIES

## SHORTBREAD

Delicious is the only word to describe these flaky and buttery shortbread cookies!

- ✓ 1 cup unbleached flour
- ✓ ¾ cup butter, softened
- ✓ ½ cup cornstarch
- ✓ ½ cup confectioners sugar

Combine the flour, cornstarch and sugar in a medium bowl. Add the butter and continue to mix until well blended. Form into one-inch balls, place on an ungreased cookie sheet and refrigerate for 30 minutes.

Pre-heat oven to 300 degrees F.

Remove the cookie sheet from the refrigerator and bake for 15-20 minutes or until a light golden color. Remove from the oven and transfer the cookies to a wire rack, paper towel or wax paper and allow to cool.

Makes 2 dozen cookies.

## PEANUT BUTTER

You don't need a lot of ingredients to prepare delicious peanut butter cookies!

- ✓ 1 cup creamy peanut butter
- ✓ ¾ cup white sugar, divided
- ✓ ½ cup light brown sugar
- ✓ 1 egg, beaten

Pre-heat oven to 350 degrees F.

Combine the peanut butter, ½ cup of white sugar, brown sugar and egg, mixing until well blended.

Form into one-inch balls and roll in remaining sugar. Place the sugared balls on an ungreased cookie sheet.

Bake for 10-12 minutes, or until a light golden color. Allow the cookies to cool before transferring to a wire rack, wax paper or paper towel.

Makes 2 dozen cookies

## LEMON DROP COOKIES

These creamy lemon cookies are delicious and so easy to prepare, you will definitely want to double the batch!

- ✓ 1 pkg. lemon cake mix
- ✓ 2 cups heavy whipping cream
- ✓ 1 egg
- ✓ ½ cup confectioners sugar

Pre-heat oven to 350 degrees F.

Combine the cake mix with the whipping cream, egg and confections sugar and mix until well blended.

Drop by a Tablespoon onto an ungreased cookie sheet.

Bake for 10-15 minutes or until a light golden color. Allow the cookies to cool before transferring to a wire rack, wax paper or paper towel.

**VARIATION:** Replace the lemon cake mix with chocolate cake mix. Follow the directions stated above.

Makes 3 dozen cookies

## PECAN SURPRISE COOKIES

These delicious cookies require no flour or eggs, and are so sweet and delicious, the whole family will love them!

- ✓ 12 oz. semi-sweet chocolate chips
- ✓ 14 oz. sweetened condensed milk
- ✓ 14 oz. sweetened coconut flakes
- ✓ 1/3 cup chopped pecans

Pre-heat oven to 350 degrees F.

Line a baking sheet with parchment paper.

Combine the chocolate chips with the condensed milk, coconut flakes and chopped pecans, mixing until well combined.

Using a tablespoon, drop the dough onto the prepared baking sheet.

Bake for 10-12 minutes. Allow the cookies to cool before transferring to a wire rack, wax paper or paper towel.

**VARIATION:** Replace the semi-sweet chocolate chips with 12 oz. of butterscotch chips and the chopped pecans with 1/3 cup of finely chopped walnuts. Follow the directions stated above.

Makes 3 dozen cookies.

## DOUBLE CHOCOLATE COOKIES

These cookies are oh so chocolaty and delicious, just watch them disappear!

- ✓ 1 box of Devil's Food Cake Mix
- ✓ ½ cup vegetable oil
- ✓ 2 eggs
- ✓ 6 oz. semi-sweet chocolate chips

Pre-heat oven to 350 degrees F.

Combine the cake mix with the vegetable oil and eggs, mixing well. Stir in the chocolate chips.

Drop by a rounded teaspoon onto an ungreased cookie sheet.

Bake for 10-15 minutes. Allow the cookies to cool before transferring to a wire rack, wax paper or paper towel.

**VARIATION:** Replace the Devil's Food cake with Red Velvet Cake Mix and the semi-sweet chocolate chips with 6 oz. of dark chocolate chips. Follow the directions stated above.

Makes 3 dozen cookies.

## VINTAGE BUTTER COOKIES

While these cookies bake and my kitchen fills with a delicious smell, it brings back childhood memories of long, lazy summer afternoons and tall glasses of fresh, cold milk!

- ✓ 1 cup butter, softened
- ✓ 2/3 cup sugar
- ✓ 1 Tablespoon vanilla extract
- ✓ 2 ¼ cup unbleached flour

Pre-heat oven to 375 degrees F.

Cream together the butter and sugar until well combined. Stir in the vanilla and then add the flour, continuing to mix until all of the ingredients are well combined.

Roll into 1-inch balls and place on an ungreased cookie sheet.

Bake for 15-18 minutes. Allow the cookies to cool before transferring to a wire rack, wax paper or paper towel.

**VARIATION:** Replace the vanilla extract with almond extract, following the directions stated above.

Makes 3 dozen cookies.

# Contents

Breakfast ............................................................... 3
Snacks from the oven.......................................... 9
Snacks on the go.................................................. 15
Harvest fruit dishes ........................................... 21
Kid-friendly salads ............................................. 27
Favorite pasta .................................................... 33
One dish meals.................................................... 39
Just for kids........................................................ 45
Cookies................................................................ 51

Made in the USA
Middletown, DE
11 September 2020